Schriever Space Force Base

Through Time

JOSEPH T. PAGE II

America Through Time®
ADDING COLOR TO AMERICAN HISTORY

This book is dedicated to the men and women of Falcon Air Force Station, for taking the first steps into operationalizing the final frontier.

America Through Time is an imprint of Fonthill Media LLC
www.through-time.com
office@through-time.com

Published by Arcadia Publishing by arrangement with Fonthill Media LLC
For all general information, please contact Arcadia Publishing:
Telephone: 843-853-2070
Fax: 843-853-0044
E-mail: sales@arcadiapublishing.com
For customer service and orders:
Toll-Free 1-888-313-2665

www.arcadiapublishing.com

First published 2022

ISBN 978-1-63499-415-6

Typeset in Mrs Eaves XL Serif Narrow
Printed and bound in England

Contents

Acknowledgments

Foremost, I would like to thank my wife and children. While my prior military experience moves further into the past, my family humors me during these brief trips into reverie.

Thanks to Mr. Donald "Jay" Prichard for helping to connect the dots with the operationalization of space from its early Cold War days to the present. I really miss the barbecues and conversations about space history under the California skies.

Thanks to Warren Pierce for the historic documents about the Satellite Control Network, and Dr. Dwayne Day for the DSCS photos from the STS-51J mission.

Immense gratitude to Alan Sutton, president of Fonthill Media. Alan took another chance, allowing me to tell the wonderful story of such a critically important (yet relatively unknown) place.

I would also like to acknowledge many unnamed Falcon space operators for their early stories of their time at "Falcatraz" and riding the icy roads of Highway 94 back when there was literally nothing out on the plains east of Colorado Springs.

Thanks to Mr. James Mesco and Mr. Randy Saunders for their work as historians for the 50th Space Wing. Their daily grind helped build the voluminous archive of information about the base and its history, and the weekly history quizzes brought the past alive for young space operators.

Finally, a long-overdue thanks to Mr. Rollan "Yoke" Yocum. During an obscure temporary duty assignment to Schriever AFB, Yoke taught this young space and missile lieutenant the true meaning of integrating space operations into the terrestrial battlespace. While I did not employ those lessons in combat, I never forgot Yoke's dedication to training the next generation of space warriors.

Introduction

Bernard Adolph Schriever

Born in Germany September 14, 1910, Bernard was the son of Adolph, a German merchant marine engineering officer, and Elizabeth, a domestic worker and later, successful business owner. During the outbreak of World War I, Adolph was interned in New York, and the young mother and her two sons—Bernard and Gerhard—emigrated from Holland to the United States in 1917 to join him, shortly before the United States declared war on Germany. With anti-German sentiment growing, the family settled in New Braunfelds, Texas, with its large German-speaking community, later moving to San Antonio. Bernard Schriever became a naturalized U.S. citizen in 1923 and subsequently attended Texas A&M University.

As part of the student body at Texas A&M, Schriever, along with the all-male student population, was enrolled in the Reserve Officer Training Corps (ROTC), wore a military uniform to class, and marched in formation to every meal. Upon graduation in 1931, Schriever earned a reserve commission in the artillery. With a boyhood fascination with flying stoked by close proximity to Kelly Field, an Army Air Corps pilot training base, Schriever applied to flight school in late 1931. Upon graduation, Second Lieutenant Schriever moved to March Field, California, flying B-4 and B-10 bombers under the command of then Lieutenant Colonel Henry H. "Hap" Arnold (1886–1950), who would later become chief of the Air Corps (1938–1941).

One early experience that colored Schriever's faith in technology was his experience in the army's experiment delivering the nation's mail via airplanes. During what would later be known as the "airmail fiasco," army aviators flew domestic airmail in O-38s and B-4s, with aircraft and crews inadequately prepared for instrument flying through hazardous routes and poor winter weather. Sixty-six crashes occurred between September 1933 and June 1934, killing twelve Army Air Corps pilots. The overwhelming failure to provide adequate training or modernize technology for the airmen remained with Schriever throughout his career.

Stints as a test pilot, engineering school graduate, bomber pilot, and maintenance officer took Schriever through World War II. These experiences would serve him well when he later became an "evangelist" for developing new technologies for use within the United States Air Force (USAF). As commander of the Air Force Ballistic Missile Division beginning in 1954, Schriever was charged with developing an intercontinental ballistic missile (ICBM) and the organization, equipment, launch sites, and facilities to support the ICBM mission, before the Soviet Union developed their missile capability.

General Schriever later commanded the USAF's Air Research and Development Command (ARDC), which became Air Force Systems Command in 1961. Directing the service's "Project Forecast," to predict the future of warfare, Schriever investigated the refinement of technologies, resulting in dramatic improvements within areas such as air and space weapon systems, information processing, composite materials, and space developments to name a few. After his retirement in 1966, Schriever continued to serve as a leader and advisor in defense applications of science and technology. As a rare show of acknowledgement for a living legend, the USAF renamed Falcon Air Force Base (AFB) on June 5, 1998, to Schriever AFB, the only military base to be named for a living individual. General Schriever's life and accomplishments are too voluminous to be adequately covered here. Interested readers are directed to Pulitzer Prize-winner Neil Sheehan's 2009 biography of Schriever, *A Fiery Peace in a Cold War*.

Nexus of Two Problems

The ostensible origins of Schriever Space Force Base (SFB) can be traced to two major issues faced by the Air Force Satellite Control Facility (AFSCF) in Sunnyvale, California. The first concern was the technological and growth limitations of the AFSCF and its satellite control network. Designed in the late 1950s, the worldwide satellite command and control network (later known as the Air Force Satellite Control Network or AFSCN) continuously supported civil, military, and national security spacecraft throughout the decades. The network's origins began as part of the National Reconnaissance Office's (NRO) Corona reconnaissance satellite program, with each successive generation of reconnaissance satellites (Gambit, Gambit-3, Hexagon, Earpop, and Kennen to name a few) using the network for commanding and on-orbit control. When the Satellite Test Center (STC or "Stick") was built in Sunnyvale in the early 1960s, it was located adjacent to Lockheed's Plant One amid a few hundred acres of fruit groves.

In the mid-1970s, technological innovation in the Bay Area had a boomtown effect on Sunnyvale, with high-tech companies razing the fruit orchards and building factories and offices. The AFSCF reached the apex of its footprint in the early 1970s after the Advance Satellite Test Center—colloquially known as the "Blue Cube" for its distinct design and color scheme—was completed in 1969. Internal upgrades to infrastructure, hardware, and software would help the AFSCF keep pace technologically, but critical vulnerabilities to sabotage and earthquake damage necessitated the need for a back-up satellite command and control facility.

The second issue facing the USAF was the creation of the Space Transportation System in the early 1970s, commonly known as the "space shuttle." The drive to get military men into space via the Manned Orbiting Laboratory (MOL) program ended unceremoniously in June 1969. The MOL was a cover program for the KH-10 reconnaissance system, in essence a "manned reconnaissance satellite" for high resolution photographic intelligence. Cancellation of the MOL came one month before the National Aeronautics and Space Administration's (NASA) Apollo program landed on the Moon, based primarily on budget cuts brought on by the war in Vietnam and development of an electro-optical (digital) satellite that could provide near-real time imagery of denied areas.

The Nixon administration's follow-up to Apollo was the creation of a "space truck" that would ferry astronauts and payloads into low-Earth orbit for short-duration missions of satellite deployment and retrieval. NASA's post-Apollo budget cuts and the USAF's continuing requirement to launch military and NRO payloads into space forced an uneasy compromise: NASA would run the shuttle program and the Department of Defense (DoD) would support launches. While the DoD's launch requirements guided the agency into requesting a military-only "Blue Shuttle," another programmatic compromise gave the military a number of reserved shuttle flights and funding to convert a former MOL facility at Vandenberg—Space Launch Complex Six—for polar-orbiting shuttle launches. The above compromises turned into a "blood pact" after the signature of National Security Decision Directive 8 (NSDD-8) by President Ronald Reagan in 1981, directing:

> The Space Transportation System will be the primary space launch system for both United States military and civil government missions. In coordination with NASA, the Department of Defense will assure the Shuttle's utility to defense and integrate national security missions into the Shuttle system.

Consolidated Space Operations Center

In the mid-1970s, the USAF began planning for the increase of military space requirements with a second satellite operations facility to share the increasing workload. This center was originally dubbed "STC-II," but became known as the Satellite Operations Complex (SOC). Due to behind-the-scenes machinations between NASA, DoD, and NRO for the shuttle to launch national security (reconnaissance) payloads, a cavalcade of responsibilities supporting the shuttle program were thrust upon the Air Force. During briefings presented to Secretary of the Air Force Thomas C. Reed on December 7–9, 1976, three alternative courses of action regarding the space shuttle were presented:

1. Modify NASA's Johnson Space Center in Houston, Texas
2. Expand the AFSCF in Sunnyvale, California
3. Constructed an all-new DoD facility, dubbed "STS Operations and Planning Center" (SOPC), at a to-be-determined (TBD) location.

The 1977 Space Mission Control Study conducted by the Space and Missile Systems Organization (SAMSO) looked at consolidating the functions of the STC, STC-II, and the Global Positioning System (GPS) control station. A 1978 study by the office of the secretary of defense (OSD)'s Satellite Control Capabilities Steering Group stated that eliminating reliance on a single control note (i.e. AFSCF) would provide survivability during wartime. Air Force Systems Command performed STC-II site surveys from May 1–12, 1978, at six potential locations: Kirtland, Hill, Mountain Home, Nellis, Luke, and Malmstrom AFBs.

In February 1979, the office of management and budget requested the DoD and NASA evaluate whether a joint mission control center or separate DOD and NASA facilities should be used to meet post-1985 space shuttle mission requirements. The result of this evaluation was a recommendation to establish a separate DOD facility that would provide a higher degree of security for military space shuttle missions. This facility was dubbed the Shuttle Operations and Planning Center (SOPC).

The addition of shuttle planning and control to the STC-II mission led to the creation of a consolidated work location—the Consolidated Space Operations Center (CSOC)—consisting of the SOC (for satellite control) and SOPC (for shuttle operations). The SOC would share responsibility with the Sunnyvale-based AFSCF for satellite command and control through the AFSCN, providing a hot-backup in times of crisis.

A Post-*Challenger* Reality

On January 28, 1986, the space shuttle *Challenger* was destroyed seventy-three seconds after lift-off over the Florida coast. The accident investigation into the causes of *Challenger*'s destruction brought many concerns into the public record. One concern—the overly optimistic shuttle launch schedule—highlighted a gaping vulnerability in the U.S. launch capability of national security satellites brought on by the Reagan administration's NSDD-8 edicts. One accident—such as *Challenger*—could derail an intricately plotted schedule for entire satellite programs, as was the case with the Navstar GPS constellation.

The realization that astronauts were not required to deploy orbital payloads also steered the USAF away from planning future military-only missions on the shuttle. Except for specific payloads constructed for Shuttle launch only, remaining satellites were scheduled onto expendable boosters such as Titan, Atlas, or Delta rockets. The DoD ostensibly killed SOPC on January 29, 1987, one year and one day after *Challenger*, by zeroizing its funding. The facilities at Falcon AFS, however, were redistributed into the burgeoning satellite control mission, allowing additional space and computing power for military satellite missions.

First Space War(s)

The 1991 Gulf War (Operation Desert Storm) was dubbed the "First Space War" by the coalition forces' skillful use of communications, imagery intelligence, tactical missile warning, weather, and navigation satellites. All of these missions involved Falcon AFB in some way, whether by direct commanding or indirect support via the AFSCN.

In 1998, the USAF recognized the impact of space on military operations and honored General Bernard Schriever by renaming Falcon AFB after him. The ongoing "trial by fire" for satellite crews continued on throughout the 1990s and early 2000s with Operations Northern and Southern Watch, Desert Fox, and ultimate conflicts in Iraqi Freedom (OIF) and Enduring Freedom (OEF). Schriever-based crews provided 24/7 access to information to warfighters in the air, land, and sea via satellite technology.

United States Space Force

With the warfighting dependence on space only increasing, as shown during the last wars of the twentieth century as well as the first conflicts of the twenty-first, the 2001 Space Commission argued for the creation of a Space Corps, a dedicated cadre of personnel entrusted to providing access to space. This idea faltered until the introduction of the United States Space Force Act on December 20, 2019, as part of the 2020 National Defense Authorization Act, reorganizing Air Force Space Command into the United States Space Force. Schriever AFB was subsequently renamed Schriever Space Force Base on July 26, 2021, cementing its importance to the United States' goal of exploring and exploiting the Final Frontier.

Today, Schriever Space Force Base has become the nexus of space command and control for the United States and its allies, a fitting legacy for the "Father of the Air Force's Ballistic Missile and Space Programs."

Author's Note

Some details on Schriever SFB's operational missions have been omitted or changed, reflecting sourcing from declassified or releasable documents to protect operational security (OPSEC) of both personnel and the systems they operate. Photographs have been sourced from the National Archives, Air Force Historical Research Agency, the National Reconnaissance Office, and United States Air/Space Force websites.

1

General Bernard A. Schriever

SECOND LIEUTENANT BENNIE SCHRIEVER, ARTILLERYMAN THEN AVIATOR: Commissioned in 1931 as a second lieutenant in the still-horse-drawn field artillery, Schriever would joke his legs were too long for horse stirrups. He applied for flying school in 1932 and took a pay cut becoming an aviation cadet, before earning a second commission as an U.S. Army Air Corps aviator on June 29, 1933. Above right, a young Lieutenant Schriever wears the aviator's uniform, complete with a leather helmet and goggles. During Schriever's first assignment at March Field, California, he would meet Lieutenant Colonel Henry "Hap" Arnold, an influential mentor and future chief of the U.S. Army Air Forces. (*United States Air Force*)

Expert in Ballistic Projectiles: Learning the game as a boy, Schriever excelled at golf throughout his formative years. Building an impressive resume on the green, Schriever won the Texas junior amateur championship and San Antonio city championship in 1931, and the city tournament again in 1932 before attending flying school. Below, then-Major General Bernard Schriever shakes hands with Dr. Simon Ramo of the Ramo-Wooldridge Corporation during the dedication of the new Western Development Division facility in 1956. The Western Development Division's mission was to develop an intercontinental ballistic missile capable of carrying a nuclear warhead. From these offices, the U.S. nuclear deterrent force would gain the Thor, Atlas, Titan, and Minuteman missiles.

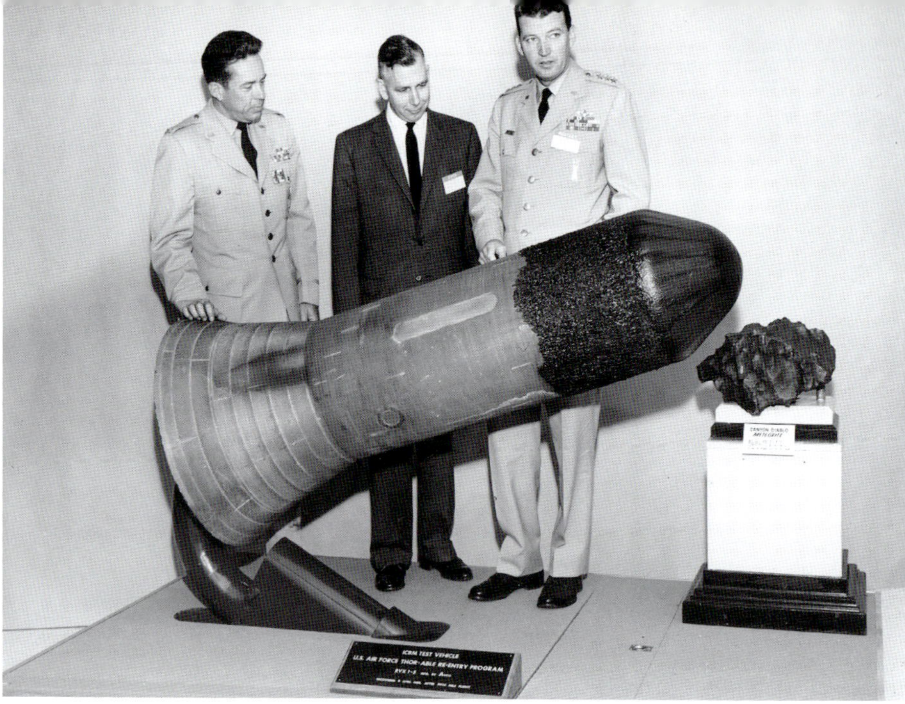

THOR'S MIGHTY REACH: Lieutenant General Schriever (far right) inspects a "used" AVCO RVX 1-5 re-entry vehicle with an unidentified military officer and civilian official. This re-entry vehicle was launched atop a Thor-Able rocket on April 8, 1959, for an approximately 5,000-mile flight over (and into) the Atlantic Ocean. The ablative nosecone reached temperatures above 12,000 degrees Fahrenheit, providing valuable data for future warhead designs. Below, Schriever watches as an American flag from Discoverer XIII is presented to President Dwight Eisenhower at the White House on August 15, 1960. The re-entry capsule from "Lucky 13" was the first manmade object returned from space, proving the concept of the Thor booster, Agena upper stage, and re-entry system. The next flight, Discoverer XIV/Corona mission 9009, provided the first photographic intelligence of the Soviet Union from space. (*United States Air Force/National Reconnaissance Office*).

DOUGLAS

PUBLISHED MONTHLY

Airview News

PROJECT EMILY — OCTOBER 1959 — No. 8

GENERAL SCHRIEVER TOURS EMILY

Lt. General Bernard Schriever, Commanding General, Advanced Research and Development Command, wore a broad smile as he toured the Project Installations recently. Accompanying the General on his inspection are from left to right: A. E. " Sarge " Willer, Field Superintendent—Project Emily; General Schriever; W. L. Duval, Thor Deployment Manager; Col. Geo. C. McDowell, 7th Air Division; W. H. Hooper, Assistant Project Engineer—Technical Operations; Lt. Col. George R. Vanden-Heuvel, Chief Technical Director, BMETO; Col. David K. Lyster, Chief —BMETO; and J. H. Sogg, Project Engineer for Emily.

OUTREACH EFFORTS, BOTH INTERNATIONAL AND DOMESTIC: In addition to being a management expert, General Schriever was also a public relations guru, understanding the connection between outreach, public opinion, and funding. In October 1959, Schriever toured Thor intermediate range ballistic missile (IRBMs) installations in the United Kingdom (above). Due to Thor's intermediate range, launch sites closer to the Soviet Union were desired. Exploiting the U.S./U.K.'s "special relationship," Thor missiles were transferred to the Royal Air Force as a hedge against Soviet aggression and as a stopgap until Atlas ICBMs matured. Below, ABC News science editor Jules Bergman interviews General Schriever in 1964 about the first decade of the U.S. missile program. Schriever continued his advocacy for space and missile programs throughout his post-military retirement years. (*Douglas Aircraft Company/United States Air Force*)

TWILIGHT OF THE FIRST GENERATION: With an erected missile in the background, General Schriever (above left) tours an Atlas-D ICBM complex in the early 1960s. Developed as the first missile system with intercontinental range in the U.S. arsenal, early Atlas systems were extremely vulnerable to nuclear attack in their above ground "coffin" launchers, as seen here. Vulnerability to enemy attack was reduced when Atlas-E and -F models were placed inside below-ground launchers. Above right, General Bruce K. Holloway (right), USAF vice chief of staff, congratulates General Schriever (left), commander of Air Force Systems Command, upon his retirement on August 31, 1966, at Andrews AFB, Maryland. (*Vandenberg Space and Missile Technology Center/United States Air Force*)

OPPOSITE PAGE

THE FATHER OF AIR FORCE SPACE AND MISSILES: Above, surrounded with scale models of rockets and missiles, the impact of General Schriever's management efforts is made evident *sans* hyperbole. First-generation missile systems such as Thor, Atlas, and Titan were often repurposed as space launch boosters for the U.S. civil, national, and military space programs. Second-generation missiles, such as the Minuteman, provided the backbone of strategic deterrence for decades. Below, Bernard Schriever stands next to his wife, Joni, on September 15, 2004, during the official groundbreaking for the future national Air Force Memorial in Washington, D.C. (*United States Air Force*)

AIR FORCE
AIR FORCE
US AIR FORCE
AIR FORCE
AIR FORCE
AIR FORCE
AIR FORCE
AIR FORCE
UNITED STATES

RECOGNIZING AMERICA'S FIRST SPACE OPERATOR: Above, General Lance Lord, commander of Air Force Space Command, presents General Bernard Schriever (retired) with the first space operations badge on May 25, 2005, at Schriever's home in Washington, D.C. The plaque (below)—with an embedded command space operations badge—stated simply "The First Badge to America's First Space Operator." (*United States Air Force*)

A LEGEND PASSES: General Bernard Adolph Schriever was buried on July 12, 2005, with full military honors at Arlington National Cemetery, Virginia. Above, his caisson was escorted by the Air Force Honor Guard and a Catholic priest to his final resting place at Section 34, Grave 162. Three T-38 Talons from the 50th Flying Training Squadron from Columbus Air Force Base, Miss., performed a flyover after he was laid to rest at the gravesite. A graveside eulogy was given by General Richard B. Myers, chairman of the joint chiefs of staff. Below, a standard Veterans Administration gravestone states his enormous legacy quite succinctly: "Father of the Air Force's Ballistic Missile & Space Programs." (*United States Air Force # 050712-F-6744C-122*)

INFLUENCING FUTURE GENERATIONS: Above, a room at the Air Force Space and Missile Museum at Cape Canaveral is dedicated to the accomplishments of General Schriever and the countless programs he influenced. On August 6, 2019, Colonel James Smith (left), 50th Space Wing commander, cuts the ribbon with retired Lieutenant Colonel Brett Schriever (right), son of General Schriever, during the grand opening of Bennie's Breakroom at Schriever AFB, Colorado. The breakroom was envisioned as a place where airmen and guardians can mentor and learn from each other while strengthening connections, all the while surrounded by a rich legacy of artifacts that reminding them of their space heritage. (*50th Space Wing Public Affairs #190806-F-UM970-0025*)

CAN'T KEEP A SCHRIEVER FROM SPACE: Major Michael Schriever (right), grandson of space pioneer General Bernard A. Schriever, observes a ceremony honoring early USAF and civilian space pioneers at Los Angeles AFB California. Then-Major Schriever was NRO's weapons and tactics chief and currently commands the 2nd Space Operations Squadron (2 SOPS) at Schriever SFB, Colorado. Below, General John Raymond, Air Force Space Command commander, receives the Schriever Space Leadership Award, presented by space pioneer General Bernard A. Schriever's great-grandson, Senior Airman Brett Schriever, during the Air Force Association's 43rd Annual Salute to SMC Banquet, on June 9, 2017. *(United States Air Force #150514-F-DC888-629/#170609-F-HW403-166)*

AN INSPIRATION TO ALL: Above, Schriever's widow, Joni James, spoke at a ceremony at the Space and Missile Systems Center dedicating a memorial to the general on November 15, 2007. The statue (below) was donated to SMC by the Air Force Association's Schriever Chapter. Behind a full-sized statue of the general looking skyward is the Wall of Honor, honoring individuals who made major contributions to the beginning, growth, and evolution of national security space and missile programs, while assigned to SMC or its predecessor organizations. (*United States Air Force #071115-F-2428H-061*)

2

OPERATIONALIZING MILITARY SPACE

Starting as part of the Agena upper stage command and control system for the Discoverer/Corona reconnaissance program, the Satellite Test Center (STC), colloquially known as the "Stick," became the world's first satellite command and control center in June 1960. Lockheed Missiles and Space Company sold the 11.4-acre plot next to their Sunnyvale Plant One facility to the USAF on November 11, 1959. Building 1001 (below) was constructed adjacent to Lockheed's production facility to share management, technical expertise, and computer resources. (*United States Air Force*)

INSIDE THE "STICK," THE FIRST SATELLITE COMMAND AND CONTROL CENTER: The STC controlled a worldwide network of satellite tracking stations that would relay commands to and from orbital spacecraft. Below, the main control room was, at the time, one of the world's most modern communication hubs. Closed-circuit television screens, orbital plotting boards, teletype systems, push-button communication panels, and two-way headsets allowed the test controller, test director, and console operators instantaneous access to teams of specialists supporting the space operations. Below, Lieutenant Colonel Charles "Moose" Mathison sits with an unidentified contractor at a satellite command console. Mathison was the commander of the USAF operations at Sunnyvale during the early days of the Discoverer/Corona Program, directing the combined military and contractor team. When Discoverer 13 (the first successful launch and capsule return) was retrieved by the navy, Mathison traveled by helicopter to the ship and brought the capsule to Hickam AFB (Hawaii) and eventually to the White House. (*United States Air Force*)

Manned Space Missions Directed from the Blue Cube: Originally conceived of as a manned, military space station, the Manned Orbiting Laboratory (MOL) (above) became the responsibility of the AFSC Space Systems Division in December 1963. In addition to his duties as AFSC commander, General Schriever became the MOL program office director in 1965. MOL's scientific intent was a cover story for the station's true purpose: a manned spy satellite designated "Dorian" (KH-10), which used humans to direct reconnaissance collection in near-real time. Below, new facilities in Sunnyvale were constructed adjacent to the existing STC. A four-story, windowless building (Bldg 1003) was constructed in 1968–1969 to contain separate command centers for MOL operations, as well as other satellite programs in the National Reconnaissance Program. The structure's light blue external paint job brought forth the nickname "The Blue Cube." MOL was cancelled in mid-1969 and the newly built facilities were used for other NRO satellite programs. (*United States Air Force*)

PHYSICAL AND EXISTENTIAL AFTERSHOCKS: Increasing mission requirements saw Air Force Satellite Control Facility (AFSCF) at Sunnyvale Air Force Station grow in importance during the late 1960s through the early 1980s. As the sole command and control site for the nation's military and reconnaissance satellites, military planners worried about security vulnerabilities inherent in the AFSCF's location and design. The 1989 Loma Prieta earthquake struck the San Francisco Bay Area on October 17, 1989, with a surface magnitude of 7.2, causing approximately $6 billion dollars (FY 89) worth of damage. Above, the earthquake damage to the Blue Cube seemingly validated the USAF's decision to build a second satellite command site in Colorado years earlier. Below, the encroachment of industry and people in Silicon Valley prevented establishment of a secure perimeter around the base and its satellite infrastructure as well as limiting future growth. (*Onizuka AFS alumni/United States Air Force*)

THE FUTURE OF THE AMERICAN SPACE PROGRAM: During the waning days of the Apollo moon program, President Nixon directed NASA to form a space task group to decide the space program's future options. In 1972, Nixon rejected plans for future missions to Mars and a lunar base for an orbiting "space truck" to ferry astronauts and satellites into low Earth orbit or to a space station (Skylab). The Space Transportation System's main draw was driving down the cost of space launches by reusing the winged gliding space vehicle (above). Due to shrinking budgets in the aftermath of the Vietnam War, NASA could not afford the space shuttle alone. Political maneuvering by both NASA and DoD created an uneasy compromise—the shuttle would be funded by civilian dollars with military support, and a promise to dedicate a number of launches to military (and NRO) payloads. To further this last point, the NRO demanded design changes to the shuttle's cargo bay dimensions to fit "[KH-9] Hexagon-sized payloads." Below, the shuttle *Enterprise* sits prior to a fit test at Space Launch Complex Six (SLC-6) at Vandenberg AFB, California, in 1985. (*Vandenberg Space and Missile Technology Center*)

West Coast Shuttle Launch and Landing Site: Selected for its unfettered access to the Pacific Ocean and possible launch trajectories for polar orbits far from populated areas, Vandenberg AFB became the West Coast shuttle launch and landing site in the mid-1970s. Above, an artist's conception of SLC-6 ("Slick Six") shows the orbiter and payload processing facilities, along with the mobile service tower and launch pad, reusing infrastructure built for the cancelled MOL program. As designed, Vandenberg AFB would receive the shuttle orbiter and satellites by air or overland travel, launch to retrieve or deploy polar-orbiting satellites, and land back at the base's approximately 15,000-foot (4580-m) long runway. Below, the nearly completed facility cost approximately $4 billion (FY85) before it was placed in minimum caretaker status after the *Challenger* disaster, killing the USAF's hopes of a "blue shuttle" with a dedicated military mission. (*National Archives*)

Space Warriors inside Cheyenne Mountain Complex (CMC): Initial construction of the North American Air Defense Command (NORAD) Combat Operations Center (COC) inside Cheyenne Mountain began on May 18, 1961. This gave military planners a command and control location survivable against long-range bombers and ballistic missiles. The complex was fully operational on April 20, 1966, with the 1st Aerospace Control Squadron (later 1st Command and Control Squadron) operating the Space Defense Center and maintaining the satellite catalog ("satcat") of earth orbiting human-made objects. In 1979, the U.S. consolidated satellite survivability, space surveillance, and anti-satellite operations inside CMC at the Space Defense Operations Center (SPADOC). Below, operators occupy SPADOC terminals, monitoring space traffic. The CMC was eliminated from CSOC basing consideration due to the disparity of mission requirements between CSOC and SPADOC: e.g. SPADOC did not perform mission planning or command generation for U.S. spacecraft, and CSOC did not maintain data on foreign space objects nor correlate indications and warning data. (*National Archives*)

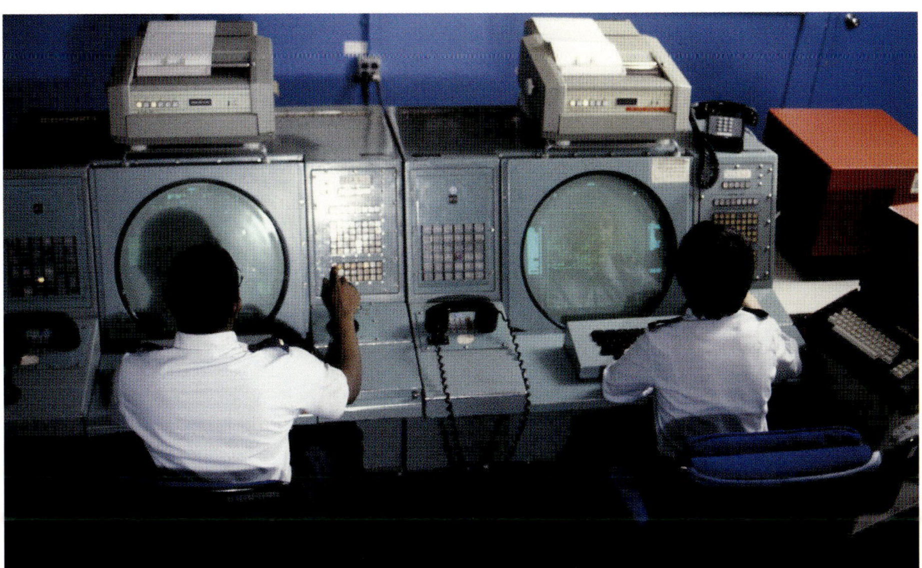

CSOC FINALISTS IN THE LAND OF ENCHANTMENT: The CSOC final basing site selection process identified three locations, including Kirtland AFB, near Albuquerque, New Mexico. Above, the preferred location for CSOC was positioned near the Manzano Foothills, immediately due east of the air base. The location capitalized on the security framework established around Manzano Base (below), and the ample acreage on the military reservation preventing urban sprawl issues faced by Sunnyvale's AFSCF. Desert climate is conducive to satellite operations, with nearly 300 days of sunshine per year and low (average) humidity. While Albuquerque was not selected based on a variety of factors, the same favorable characteristics saw NASA place their civilian CSOC-equivalent Tracking and Data Relay Satellite System (TDRSS) command sites located 180 miles south, near Las Cruces. (*National Archives*)

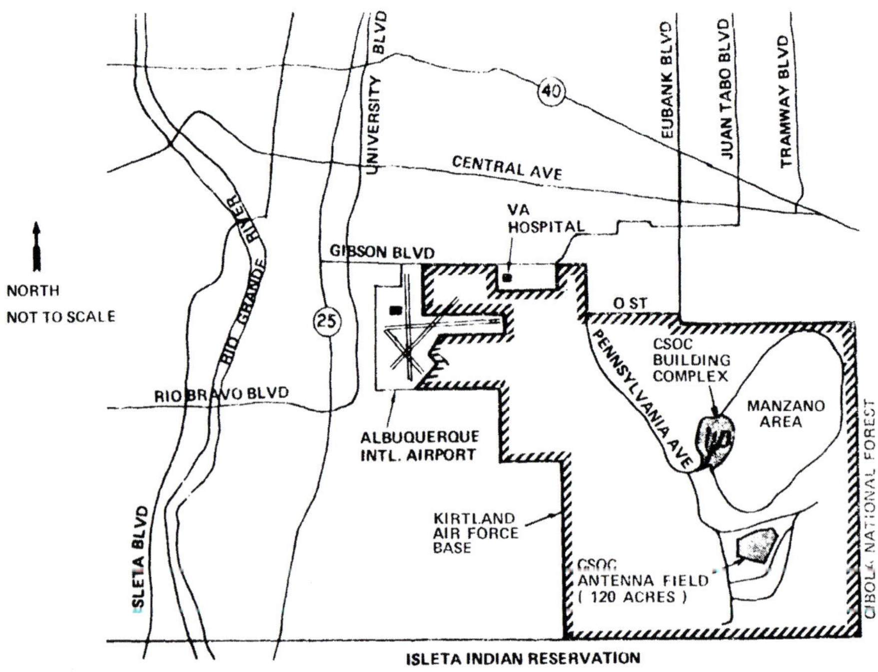

3

Building CSOC

In 1979, the secretary of the USAF (SecAF) directed three sites (Albuquerque, Great Falls, and Colorado Springs) be re-surveyed to determine the impact of CSOC operations on the military bases. The USAF Space Division determined that Luke AFB, Arizona, and Kirtland AFB, NM, were the best choices, owning to being with 250 miles of the U.S. border, a cloud-free area 70–90 percent of the time, and adequate visibility of the geostationary communications satellites. While the original site at Peterson AFB was rejected, another location 10 miles east was put forth. With Kirtland/Albuquerque and the Colorado Springs area in a dead-heat, subjective factors deemed dubious by the government accountability office were put forth as criterion. These included USAF justifications for CSOC and SPADOC being located near each other, as well as a pre-established industry base from previous air defense infrastructure. Following negotiations, Colorado state leadership granted the federal government deed to approximately 640 acres of land (above) east of Colorado Springs near the then-unincorporated town of Falcon. (*United States Air Force # 190529-F-O3755-2003*)

AN APROPOS BEGINNING FOR FALCON AFS: On May 17, 1983, Air Force Space Command leadership broke ground (above) during a snowy day on what would become Falcon Air Force Station. For more than two years, contractors worked to complete facilities, including headquarters and operations buildings, support facilities, and infrastructure as seen in the base model below. This model could easily compare to the base's outline today with the same recognizable features. (*Author's Collection*)

AERIAL VIEWS OF FALCON AFS UNDER CONSTRUCTION: Above is an aerial view of Falcon AFS looking toward the southeast as early facilities were under construction. Most noticeable is the north parking lot, the 2d Space Wing headquarters (Bldg. 500), CSOC (Bldg. 400), the site support building, and the central power plant. Below, the aerial view shows the completed headquarters building, CSOC, and industrial plant. Missing from early construction is the west parking lot, Joint National Test Facility, and additional support facilities later added over the decades. (*National Archives DF-ST-86-11255/DF-ST-88-04643*)

OPENING OF FALCON AFS AND THE JACK SWIGERT SPACE OPERATIONS FACILITY: Above, Bldg. 400 is a three-story structure housing satellite operations and containing approximately 354,000 sq. feet of workspace. In June 1986, Bldg. 400 was named to honor astronaut and Colorado Congressman-elect John "Jack" Swigert (1931–1982). Born and raised in Denver, Swigert was the command module pilot on the ill-fated Apollo 13 moon mission. Upon leaving NASA, he ran for Congress and was elected, but died one week prior to accepting office in December 1982. Below, a ribbon-cutting ceremony on September 26, 1985, marked the opening of Falcon Air Force Station. (*National Archives DF-ST-86-11257/ United States Air Force #180925-F-F3751-1001*)

INTERMINABLE LANDMARKS: Workers (above) exit the north portal into the base-controlled areas. Arriving at Falcon's two parking lots offers a unique daily ritual: finding close parking as near to the entrance as possible. The 24/7 operations tempo does not afford any "best" times to arrive and get a good parking spot, so it is all based on luck, coincidence, and knowing when squadron mates are leaving their shifts. Below, the base sign reflects the Air Force Space Command logo and designation of "air force station," *c.* November 1987. Falcon was redesignated an air force base on June 13, 1988, as part of a command-wide renaming. *(National Archives DF-ST-89-05396/ DF-ST-89-05394)*

AF BLUES INSIDE CUBICAL CITY: Above, staff areas inside the 2d Space Wing engineering and administration building show a cubical "farm" longer than a football field ready to house incoming support personnel. While television and movies glamourize space operations with fast-paced action sequences, reality presents a different image of workers inside office cubicles when not on the operations floor. Below, an unidentified Falcon airman sits in front of a computer terminal. What is noticeable about this image is her uniform: Class B "blues," akin to business casual for the civilian sector. In later years, the uniform of the day would change to "battle dress" camouflage uniforms or flight suits, altering the cadre's presentation as space warriors, not just support personnel. (*Author's Collection*)

BASE SUPPORT: POWER AND CHOW HALL: Above, First Lieutenant Leslie Cates-Blackham, member of the Falcon site activation task force, gives a tour of the Falcon dining facility. At the time of construction, the dining facility supported four meals a day and could feed 400 people at a time. Below, First Lieutenant Cates-Blackham continues her tour of the central plant with one of the six 23,000 kilovolt-amps diesel generators behind her. While the base runs primarily on commercial power, the generators provide a backup power capability in case of emergency. (*Author's Collection*)

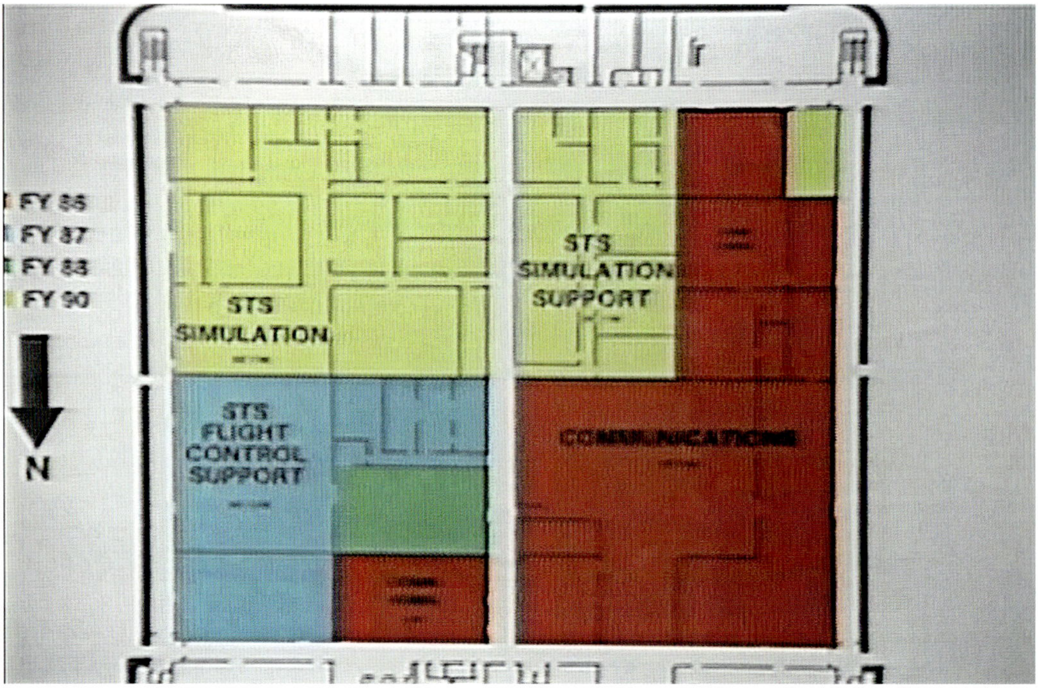

CSOC OUTLINE: Above and below show the intended outline of the CSOC footprint inside Building 400. The first floor (above) was dedicated to the SOPC, with simulation and flight control support for shuttle operations. Below, the second floor also contained shuttle support functions, with command centers for the MILSTAR communications satellite. After the demise of the shuttle's military mission, these control centers were distributed to other satellite missions supported by SOC personnel. (*Author's Collection*)

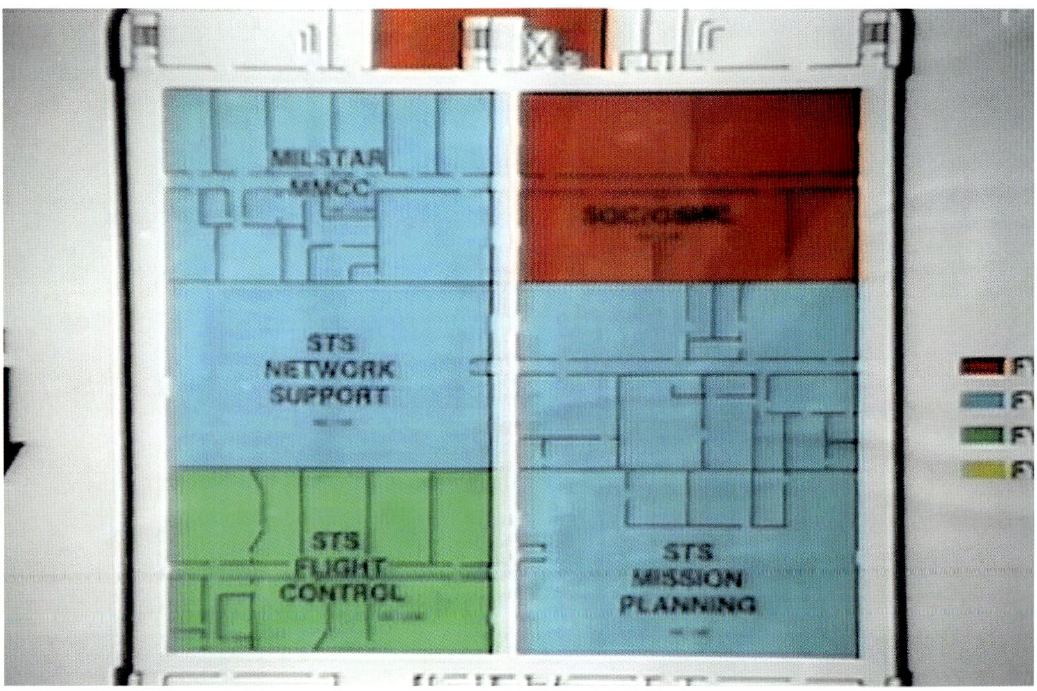

4

Falcon AFS' Early Days

The logo of the 2d Space Wing contains blue and yellow, alluding to the sky and sun respectively. The globe represents the earth as viewed from space and signifies the worldwide coverage provided by USAF satellites when accomplishing surveillance and communications missions. The ellipse symbolizes an orbital path around the Earth and the two stars depict the satellites. The deltoid and its contrail denote the USAF launch vehicles that place the satellites in orbit. The seven stars represent the vastness of space and the environment of our operations. The wing was created to provide administrative support to the various satellite control squadrons at Falcon. Due to a resurgence of interest to preserve the service's historical flying heritage after the Gulf War, the wing was replaced by the 50th Tactical Fighter Wing on January 30, 1992, becoming the 50th Space Wing. (*Air Force Historical Research Agency*)

FIRST DAYS AT FALCON: Above, 2d Space Wing commander, Colonel Richard "Larry" Griffin (1934–2020) (center), poses with his staff on July 28, 1985, weeks after the wing's initial activation. During the early years of the shuttle program, Griffin served as a liaison between the Air Force and NASA, gaining valuable experience for his subsequent command at Falcon and assumption of the (aborted) SOPC mission. Below, Captain Patricia Coomber and Second Lieutenant Kevin Carter monitor GPS satellites inside the 2d Satellite Control Squadron's (2 SCS) mission control station inside Bldg. 400. The 2 SCS was activated on October 1, 1985, for the operations and maintenance of the Navstar GPS navigation satellite constellation. (*United States Air Force/National Archives DF-ST-89-05400*)

First Satellites Controlled from Falcon AFS: Above, Captain Carla Brown (far left) sits between Captain Ricky Reese (center)—acting as mission commander—and First Lieutenant Christina Warrender (center left)—as payload analyst—directing their training on Navstar GPS procedures inside the satellite operations center. Navstar GPS was one of the first satellite constellations transferred to Falcon AFS from the AFSCF in Sunnyvale and the interim master control station at Vandenberg AFB, California. Below, Sergeant Robert A. Pharras from the 2nd Satellite Control Squadron uses an Evans and Sutherland 3D graphics computer to plot a partially filled modified Walker constellation. The first GPS constellation contained eighteen satellites in three planes, inclined to 55 degrees. This pattern guaranteed worldwide continuous coverage but proved to be too sensitive to satellite failures. (*National Archives DF-ST-93-03915/DF-ST-89-05402*)

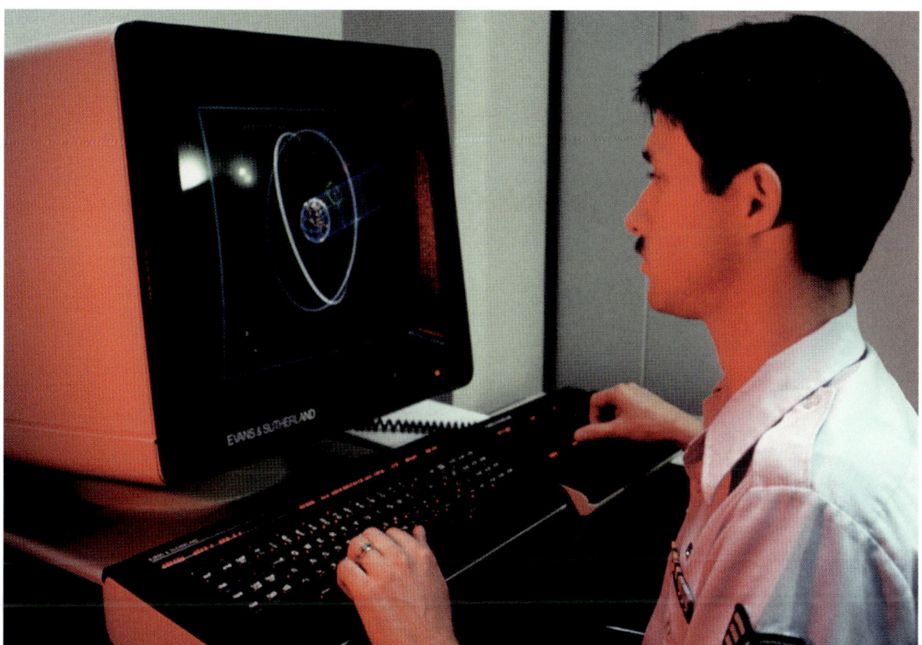

DATA STORAGE FOR CSOC OPERATIONS: Above, Staff Sergeant Jon Loehndorf changes a magnetic media tape reel onto an IBM 3420 tape drive in the CSOC main computer room on May 1, 1987. Each tape reel held data at a density of 6,250 bytes per inch over a 2400-foot reel, for a total storage of 170 megabytes per reel. The 3400 series magnetic tape units supported an "autoloader" cartridge (the white band around the edge of the reel), enabling the tape operator to mount the reel directly on the hub without having to thread the tape onto a take-up reel, providing a significant time saving while reducing operator errors. Below, Sergeant Darrell A. Harrison from the 1002d Space Systems Support Squadron selects a magnetic tape reel from a library storage rack in the SOC main computer room. (*National Archives DF-ST-93-03916/ DF-ST-89-05401*)

MUNDANE CARE AND FEEDING OF SATELLITE SUPPORT EQUIPMENT: Above, Staff Sergeant Jerry A. Robinson from the 1879th Communications Squadron checks the specific gravity in one of the batteries located in the Defense Satellite Communications System (DSCS) facility's power production room. While an impressive showing, battery banks like these can provide around fifteen minutes of backup power if primary commercial power fails, illustrating the massive power draw from computing equipment. Below, Airman First Class Dan L. Edwards uses a spectrum analyzer to monitor landline signals inside the technical control area of the DSCS facility. Communications satellites are advanced "switchboards in the sky," connecting hundreds or thousands of voice or data circuits to Earth-based terminals. (*National Archives DF-ST-89-0540/DF-ST-89-05407*)

SATCOM CONNECTIVITY FOR U.S. FORCES: Above, a pair of AN/GSC-52 antennae at Falcon provide connectivity to super high frequency (SHF) satellites within the geostationary DSCS constellation. The antenna subsystem has a 38-foot parabolic-reflector antenna, an elevation over azimuth pedestal, and a servo-drive mechanism for acquisition and auto-tracking of the satellite. Below, an artist's conception of a DSCS II satellite shows a spin-stabilized cylindrical body covered in solar cells to generate electricity. A mainstay of military satellite communications throughout the 1970s and 1980s, the last DSCS II satellite was retired in 2008. (*National Archives DF-ST-89-05403/DF-ST-83-02489*)

SHUTTLE LIFT FOR DSCS: Above left, a DSCS III satellite sits inside the cargo bay of the space shuttle *Atlantis* during mission STS-51J (October 3–7, 1985). At the time, the shuttle cargo remained a close-held secret; decades later, the dual DSCS III satellite payload was declassified. DSCS III satellites provided nuclear-hardened, anti-jam, high data rate, long haul communications to users worldwide. Above right, the emblem of the 3d Space Operations Squadron (3 SOPS) shows their mission to provide worldwide communications connectivity. After the final DSCS III (B-6) launch in 2003, 3 SOPS transitioned to the wideband gapfiller satellite (WGS), later changed to Wideband Global SATCOM. Each WGS satellite provides ten times the capacity of a DSCS III satellite. On June 13, 2017, 3 SOPS inactivated and merged its mission with the 4th Space Operations Squadron. (*Dwayne Day/Air Force Historical Research Agency*)

Falcon AFS' Direct Connection into the AFSCN: Above, Ford Aerospace senior contractor Stephen L. Gurican oversees construction on the Colorado Tracking Station, commonly known as PIKE. Prior to the construction of PIKE, the primary AFSCN control node in Onizuka AFB (CA) relied on DSCS circuits, landlines, and transportable magnetic media to interact with the worldwide remote tracking network. After PIKE's completion, the SOC had a hardwired connection into the network, with on-site hardware and personnel. Below, the prominent shelter dome protects the antenna from the elements. PIKE began communicating with military satellites in 1988 and was the only site that deployed all of the AFSCN antenna types over its lifetime. (*National Archives DF-ST-89-05399/DF-ST-89-05397*)

CONNECTING HEAVEN AND EARTH: Above, the emblem of the 22d Space Operations Squadron and its motto *Conectens Caeli Terraque* ("Connecting the Heavens and Earth") highlight the unit's mission of worldwide connectivity through the AFSCN. Activated in 1991, the squadron began as the AFSCN secondary control node, backup to the facilities at Onizuka AFB. As operations at Onizuka AFB wound down, 22 SOPS gained responsibility as the primary control node for the network. Below, PIKE's antenna sits snug inside its environmental shelter. PIKE was the first automated remote tracking station system, advancing data system modernization for the entire network, and a testbed for AFSCN upgrades being the first site to test new equipment, configurations, and capabilities. (*Air Force Historical Research Agency/National Archives DF-ST-89-05398*)

ALWAYS IN CONTROL: Above, the emblem of the 1st Space Operations Squadron (1 SOPS) states they are "Always in Control." Activated as the 1st Satellite Control Squadron on October 5, 1987, 1 SOPS assumed on-orbit support responsibilities for Navstar GPS satellites in early February 1988 and began operational commanding of defense support program (DSP) satellites later that year. Below, the cylindrical-shaped DSP satellites are a key part of North America's early warning system. In their geosynchronous orbits, DSP satellites detect missile launches, space launches, and nuclear detonations. DSP launch and early orbit support was controlled by 1 SOPS before transferring control to Buckley Air National Guard Base near Aurora, Colorado. (*Air Force Historical Research Agency/National Archives DF-SC-82-06654*)

5

The First Worldwide Utility: The Navstar Global Positioning System

An artist's conception of the Navstar global positioning system (GPS) constellation shows the proposed users in the land, air, sea, and space. During the early days of the Space Race, experiments for tracking Sputnik found that the Doppler shift of its beeping signal provided information to determine the exact moment of its closest approach to the earth. This characteristic led to the development of the Navy Navigational Satellite System (NNSS), later renamed TRANSIT, for use as a navigation aid for military aircraft and ships from 1959 to 1996. TRANSIT's success led to a follow-on experimental program, TIMATION (timed navigation) using a broadcast time reference for use as a ranging signal to receivers on the ground. TIMATION and the USAF's Project 621B formed the basis for the Navstar GPS constellation. (*National Archives DF-SC-82-06653*)

EARLY DAYS OF THE GLOBAL POSITIONING SYSTEM: Above, two U.S. Army Material Command soldiers practice navigation using information received from Block I GPS satellites in the early 1980s. The backpack holds an antenna for reception, processing electronics, and a battery, while a handheld display provided navigation coordinates to the user. Since GPS provides only ranging signals, the user electronics must calculate accurate positioning information. Below, an image shows the launching of a Block II GPS satellite from the space shuttle, with a second inside the cargo bay. Launching Block II GPS satellites was one of the primary missions for the shuttle in the 1980s, but the *Challenger* disaster pushed reconstitution of the constellation to the Delta II expendable rocket. (*National Archives DF-SC-82-10595/DF-ST-83-02552*)

PATHWAYS FOR PEACE: Above, the emblem of the 2d Space Operations Squadron (2 SOPS) prominently displays a compass rose representing Polaris, the celestial pole star, used by early navigators. Early in development, it was understood that the GPS signal would have multi-faceted users such as civil aviation and maritime. The explosion of GPS users after the 1991 Gulf War pushed the constellation into becoming the world's first global utility. Below, an artist's concept of the modified Walker constellation providing 24/7 global coverage of with Block I GPS satellites. As new satellites joined the constellation, they would be inserted into the required orbital plane to assist with signal broadcasts. Later, modifications with Block II satellites changed the orbital inclination and number of satellites in each plane. (*Air Force Historical Research Agency/National Archives DF-ST-83-02504*)

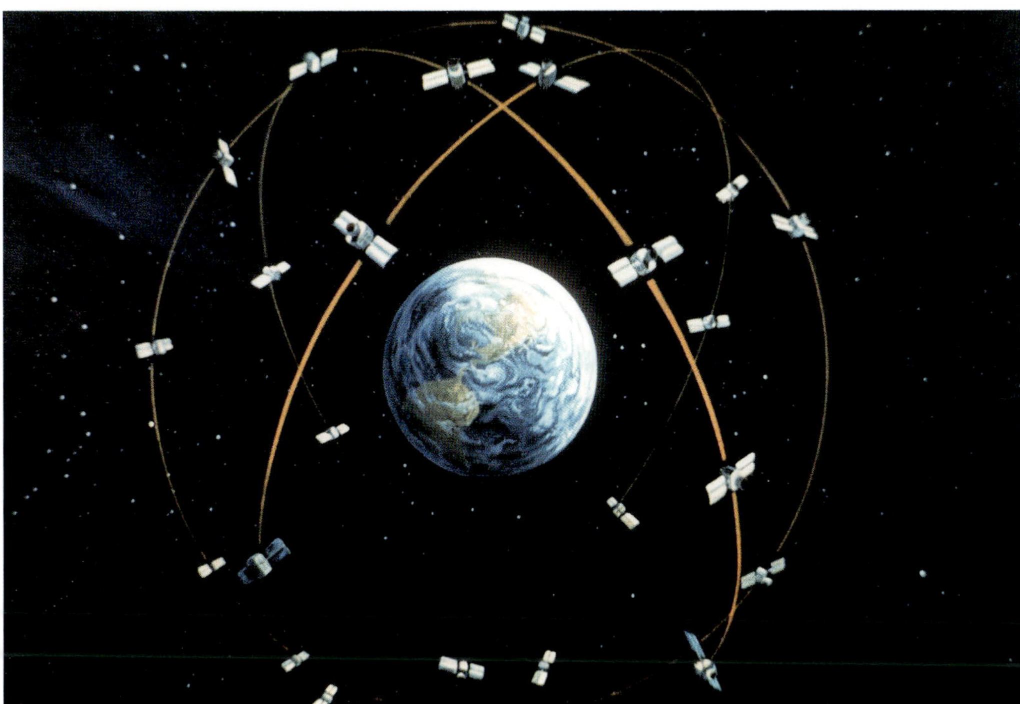

WHERE THE ACTION IS: Above, the 2 SOPS operations floor contains duty positions to provide commanding and controlling of the GPS satellite bus and maintain its navigation payload. Below, the artist's conception of a Block II GPS satellite on-orbit shows a twelve-element antenna array arranged in two concentric rings, containing eight elements in the outer ring and four in the inner ring. The spiral-wound right-hand circularly polarized (RHCP) helical antennas provide full earth coverage. (*National Archives DF-ST-98-01946/DF-SC-83-06828*)

ANSWERING THE QUESTIONS "WHERE AM I?" AND "WHAT TIME IS IT?": Above, First Lieutenant Mark Lester tests his AN/PSN-11 precision lightweight GPS receiver (PLGR) on the plains of Colorado. The PLGR was the most widely used GPS receiver in the U.S. military for over a decade. It was low cost and hand-held, allowing military members to plot their precise locations. The PLGR was introduced in March 1993, with over 200,000 units manufactured over its lifetime. Below, Captain Jennifer Kirby (left, foreground) talks with Staff Sergeant Jason Boswell in the 2 SOPS operations center during the weeks prior to the year 2000. Ensuring Y2K compliance was a high priority for the U.S. government after discovering some computer systems using two-digit year representation could misinterpret the year 2000 as 1900. *(National Archives DF-ST-98-01948/DF-SD-02-02563)*

SAYING GOODBYE TO A "FRIEND": Above, Senior Master Sergeant Blair Burdick II (center, seated) sends the last command to decommission GPS satellite vehicle number-38 (SVN-38) on October 9, 2019, while Airman First Class David Valentine (left), Boeing engineer Arturo Martínez (center, standing), and First Lieutenant Kristina Brandes (right) observe. The squadron allowed Burdick the opportunity to decommission the twenty-two-year-old satellite from service, to make way for the next-generation GPS-III satellites. Below, a signed picture of actor and singer Billy Dee Williams sits along with pre-launch images of SVN-38 at the 2 SOPS operations floor during the decommissioning. SVN-38 was nicknamed "Billy Dee" based on an internal joke. Note the inscription "To the Boys at Falcon." (*United States Air Force 191009-F-UM970-0003/191009-F-UM970-0006*)

Females in the Final Frontier: Above, Senior Airman Nayibe Ramos runs through a checklist during a satellite contact inside the 2SOPS operations center. Interactions with GPS satellites—a "contact"—can range from the routine, such as checking fuel tank temperature or the battery strength to the urgent, like when a satellite stops broadcasting a signal. And yes, during space operations there are checklists for everything. On July 23, 2020, 2 SOPS posted an all-female crew for the gaining of satellite control authority for SVN-76. *Below, from left to right*: Airman First Class Gillian Clover, First Lieutenant Alexis Thuli, Senior Airman Joelle Schritt, First Lieutenant Mary McLaughlin (center, back), First Lieutenant Kelley McCaa (center, front), First Lieutenant Mikayla Robertson, Airman First Class Larissa Contreras, and Staff Sergeant Kelly Malone. (*United States Air Force 040205-F-0000C-001/ 200723-F-WR604-0002*)

Popular Location for Distinguished Visitors, Pt 1: Above, Chief Master Sergeant of the Air Force (CMSgt) Kaleth O. Wright (left) listens as Major Matthew Miller (right) explains his role in the GPS mission on April 9, 2019. Wright saw how 2 SOPS conducts integrated and innovative operations in their mission. Below, CMSAF Joanne S. Bass sends a signal to a GPS satellite while Specialist 4 Marcus Myers (center left, standing) assists during a visit on May 5, 2021. (*United States Air Force 190409-F-UM970-0018/210505-F-WR604-0043*)

Popular Location for Distinguished Visitors, Pt 2: Above, General David L. Goldfein, chief of staff of the USAF (CSAF), listens to First Lieutenant Mark Skinner, 2 SOPS GPS mission commander, explain current 2 SOPS activities during his visit on December 20, 2016. Goldfein toured various squadrons across the base during his visit, receiving in-person briefings and engaging with airmen. During Operation Allied Force, then-Lieutenant Colonel Goldfein was shot down in his F-16 by a Serbian S-125 missile on May 2, 1999. Goldfein evaded his pursuers and was rescued by USAF pararescue assisted by GPS technology. Below, Vice President Mike Pence sits at a 2 SOPS command console while surrounded by then-Air Force General John Raymond (right), Secretary of the Air Force Heather Wilson (center, standing) and others during a visit to Schriever AFB on June 23, 2017. (*United States Air Force 161220-F-JY173-029/170623-F-JY173-0033*)

Does Anybody Really Know What Time It Is?: Above, Mathematician Jim Skinner discusses the accuracy of the world's second most accurate clock for a U.K.-based film crew for the Discovery Channel on August 7, 2007. The U.S. Naval Observatory (USNO) is charged with the responsibility for precise time determination and management of time dissemination for the United States. The alternate master clock (AMC), seen below, is synchronized with the USNO's master clock in Washington, D.C. within 2–3 nanoseconds. The AMC consists of three hydrogen masers, twelve cesium-beam frequency standards, their associated measurement and distribution systems, and several GPS time transfer receiver systems. Although the purpose of the AMC is to provide precise time in the event of a catastrophic failure of the USNO master clock, its role has expanded to include providing precise time to the GPS constellation operated from Schriever. *(United States Air Force 070807-F-9523M-054/060104-F-3966R-005)*

6

Schriever's Space Warriors

The emblem of the 50th Space Wing originated with the 50th Tactical Fighter Wing (50 TFW) and its Cold War antecedents. Operating from Hahn Air Base in West Germany for nearly four decades, the 50 TFW became the first USAF overseas unit to operate the F-16 Fighting Falcon in 1981. Deploying for the Persian Gulf War of 1991, the 50 TFW was inactivated later that year, yet was resurrected as a space wing on January 30, 1992, replacing the 2d Space Wing. (*Air Force Historical Research Agency*)

COLONEL DEKOK TAKES COMMAND: Above, members of the official party stand during the activation of the 50th Space Wing on January 30, 1992. *From left to right*: Lieutenant General Thomas Moorman, commander of Air Force Space Command; Colonel Roger DeKok, incoming 50th Space Wing commander; Colonel George Norwood, the last commander of the 50 TFW; and Chief Master Sergeant Albriey Forte, 50th Space Wing senior enlisted advisor. Below, Lieutenant General Moorman hands the wing guidon to Colonel DeKok, signifying the organization's change of command. (*United States Air Force 190129-F-F3751-1001/180628-F-QZ963-1001*)

FALCON'S AFS AND THE STRATEGIC DEFENSE INITIATIVE: Above, Lieutenant General Thomas S. Moorman Jr., commander-in-chief, Air Force Space Command, escorts Air Force Chief of Staff General Merrill A. McPeak as he arrives for a tour of Falcon's facilities during the post-Persian Gulf War period on July 3, 1991. Another large program brought to the base in the late 1980s was the strategic defense initiative's national test bed (NTB), an effort to test and evaluate a proposed strategic defense system against ballistic missiles. Falcon's joint national test facility formed the nucleus of the NTB network evaluating battle management system architectures and assisted in missile detection and tracking during the Gulf War. Below, visitors stand outside the joint national test facility during a visit in March 1999. *From left to right*: U.S. Navy Captain John J. Hammerer Jr., commander joint national test facility; Senator Robert Smith (R-NH); Senator Mary Landrieu (D-LA); General Richard Myers, commander-in-chief, North American Aerospace Defense Command; and Brigadier General William R. Looney III, commander of the Space Warfare Center. (*National Archives DF-SC-92-08649/DF-SD-01-08174*)

SPACE WARFARE—THE NEXT GENERATION: In late 1992, an USAF blue ribbon panel on space recommended establishing a dedicated Space Warfare Center to exploit the capabilities of space-based assets. Combat operations during the Persian Gulf War relied on space support more than in any previous conflict, while still identifying serious shortfalls in the ability to leverage space capabilities. In order to better exploit space capabilities, the Space Warfare Center was stood-up at Schriever AFB and officially dedicated on November 1, 1993. Below, Staff Sergeant Jeff A. Reasoner establishes communication through an INMARSAT satellite telephone during field exercises in June 1996. Practical usage of commercial space capabilities such as INMARSAT boosted knowledge of how and when these systems can be used during crises or combat, for both friendly and adversary forces. (*Air Force Historical Research Agency/National Archives DF-ST-98 01949*)

PLANNING AGAINST (AND WITH) THE ADVERSARY: Above, Captain Mark Lester briefs Chairman of the Joint Chiefs of Staff General John M. Shalikashvili (1936–2011) on the operations of the USAF space support teams as part of the 76th Space Operations Squadron. AFSSTs provided in-theater space expertise to unified warfighting commanders via situational awareness tools that provided signals intelligence, secondary imagery dissemination, overlaying potential threats onto two-dimensional navigation charts or multi-spectral images. Embedded AFSST members would ensure that command and control, communications, weather, navigation, and other space assets were used effectively multiply space-borne capabilities against an adversary. Below, General Colonel Viktor Miruk, first deputy commander-in-chief, Russian Federation Air Defense Forces (leaning over the keyboard) and General Lieutenant Nikolai Zaitsev (standing directly behind) along with other Russian officers and enlisted members, participate in a theater missile defense command post exercise on March 17, 1999. (*National Archives DF-SC-98-02633/DF-SC-98-05192*)

DISTINGUISHED VISITORS MEET THE TROOPS: Above, Senator Ben "Nighthorse" Campbell (R-CO) (left) and Air Force General Richard B. Myers (Right), commander in chief, North American Aerospace Defense Command, pose with Senior Airman Stacy Woodward of the 50th Security Forces Squadron (50 SFS) at Schriever AFB. While oft neglected in the press, security forces hold a critical role in the defense of the people and resources at Schriever AFB. Below, Air Force Chief of Staff General Michael Ryan enjoys lunch while conversing with the airmen at the joint national test facility dining hall on September 1, 1999. (*National Archives DF-SD-01-08218/ DF-SD-01-08222*)

PEOPLE AND PARTNERSHIPS MAKE SCHRIEVER AFB: Above, German Air Force Lieutenant General Peter A. Vogler visits with Colonel Rails Ryals in the Space Warfare Center's war room at Schriever AFB in February 1999. International exchanges such as these helps solidify intent and cooperation during orbital activities. Consensus among nations rates as a service priority due to the orbital regime's inherent nature as a global common. Below, Colonel James Ross, 50 SW commander, and Chief Master Sergeant Brad Shirley, 50 SW acting command chief, lead the team Schriever formation during the Colorado Springs Veteran's Day Parade, November 5, 2011. (*National Archives DF-SD-01-08377/United States Air Force 111105-F-XT791-364*)

MILSTAR CONNECTING THE FORCES WORLDWIDE: Above, the Milstar (formerly an acronym for "Military Strategic and Tactical Relay") satellite provides the president, secretary of defense, and the U.S. armed forces with assured, survivable satellite communications with low probability of interception and detection. The objective of the Milstar program was to create a global, secure, nuclear-survivable, space-based communication constellation, with all communication processing and network routing onboard, thus eliminating the need for vulnerable land-based relay stations. This global connectivity mission is reflected, below, on the 4th Space Operations Squadron (4 SOPS) emblem and with the motto "Linking the Forces." (*United States Air Force/Air Force Historical Research Agency*)

Bringing DOOM to a Battlefield Near You: Above, Captain James Spindler, 4 SOPS director of operations mobile operations unit, secures the perimeter while other 4 SOPS DOOM personnel load the mobile asset into the back of a C-17 at Peterson AFB on October 5, 2010. The mobile trucks allow crews to perform command and control of advanced extremely high frequency (AEHF) satellites, the satellite replacement for the aging Milstar system. Below, Senior Airman Anna Welby signs the mural she painted in the 4 SOPS hallway on April 7, 2009. The mural depicts the Milstar satellite, and the AEHF satellite, both flown by 4 SOPS. *(United States Air Force 101310-F-6354P-006/090407-F-6113F-011)*

KNOW, TEACH, REPLICATE: Above, Technical Sergeant Ted Meinert (left), 527th Space Aggressor Squadron (527 SAS) technical lead, configures a scanner while Captain Chris "Crisco" Todd (right, in flight suit), 527 SAS mission commander, verifies frequencies. The 527 SAS trained C-130 aircrews from the 29th Weapons Squadron at Little Rock AFB (AR) on recognizing GPS jamming and reacting appropriately. Below, the 527 SAS and 26 SAS emblems are painted side by side on doors inside the Space Aggressors' facility, highlighting the Total Force cooperation from active duty and the reserves. The Space Aggressors replicate live GPS and SATCOM electronic attack for training audiences across the globe. (*United States Air Force 060501-F-0000T-001/160712-F-NG695-003*)

EXCELLENCE IN ALL WE DO: Above, Lieutenant Colonel Scott "Lucky" Bonzer, 527 SAS commander (center standing), and Captain Mark "Reaper" Crimm (left standing) monitor Technical Sergeant Steven "Trench" St. John (center), and Staff Sergeant Christopher Bouma operates SATCOM equipment inside the squadron's operations area. Technical Sergeant St. John, 527 SAS Weapons and Tactics Flight NCO-in-charge, was named the 2013 USAF enlisted space systems operator of the year award for his space expertise, leadership, and comportment. Below, Technical Sergeant Josh Cobb, 527th Space Aggressor Squadron adversary training flight chief, explains the mission of the 527 SAS to Congressman Douglas Lamborn (R-CO) during a visit to the squadron on April 1, 2015. Cobb was a previous recipient of the 14th Air Force airman of the year. (*United States Air Force 140411-F-OT300-001/150401-F-527SA-001*)

BEST OF THE BEST COMPETE AT GUARDIAN CHALLENGE: Above, members of the 50 SFS hold up their mascot "The General" (Senior Airman Lee Heineken) upon arrival at Vandenberg AFB, California, for Guardian Challenge 2004 as 50 SW commander Colonel Suzanne M. Vautrinot (far right, green flight suit) looks on. The four-day space and missile competition tested the wartime readiness of Air Force Space Command professionals, from operations to security forces to maintenance and support. Below, 50 SW competitors pose for a group photo after winning the Aldridge Trophy as the best satellite operations unit, during Guardian Challenge 2002, at Vandenberg AFB on May 9, 2002. The Aldridge Trophy is named for former Secretary of the Air Force (and Director of the National Reconnaissance Office) Edward C. "Pete" Aldridge. Aldridge was also slated to be on the first polar-orbiting mission from SLC-6, directly tying into the base's support from SOPC. Alas, the destruction of *Challenger* pulled Aldridge from consideration for future shuttle missions. (*National Archives DF-SD-06-12430/DF-SD-04-06668*)

Running the Gauntlet: Above, members of the 50 SFS are congratulated by Colonel Diann Latham (center, left), 50th Space Wing competition commander, after completing the obstacle course during Guardian Challenge 2002. While operations personnel are tested in their computer environments, security forces personnel are tested "in the elements," with shooting, running, climbing against teams from other USAF space units. Below, the 50 SW mascot, a fictitious Union Civil War "General Palmer," makes a grand entrance at the Guardian Challenge awards kick-off ceremony attempting to pump up the crowd. Each wing organization sends their mascots to Guardian Challenge to represent their "home team" and engage in playful yet boisterous challenges against other mascots. (*National Archives DF-SD-04-06641/DF-SD-06-02185*)

PIKE NEARS END-OF-LIFE: Above, Lieutenant Colonel Scott Angerman (right), 22d Space Operations Squadron commander, presents a plaque to Ken Lavoie (center), representing PIKE's satellite operators as Technical Sergeant Shale Norwitz (far left) looks on during the Colorado tracking station's cessation ceremony from the AF satellite control network on August 3, 2012. Fittingly, PIKE's first and final operational contacts were with the Navstar GPS constellation. The station transitioned to test support role until its deactivation in 2014. Below, a commemorative cake lists PIKE's achievements during its cessation ceremony. (*United States Air Force 120803-F-WR604-044/120803-F-WR604-047*)

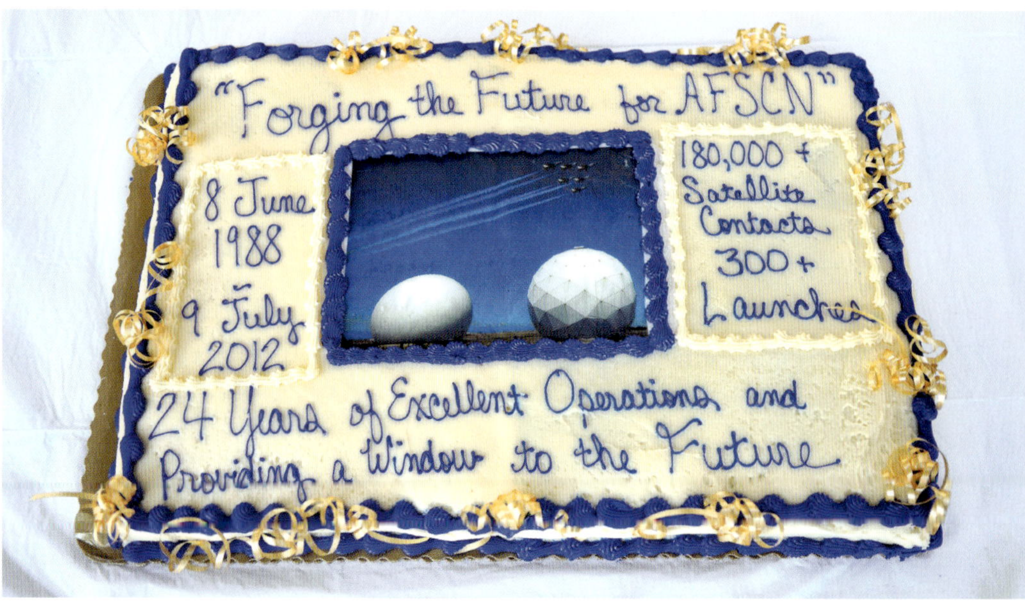

Farewell to the Colorado Tracking Station: Above, one of PIKE's antenna buildings was demolished on September 19, 2014, ten days before the official decommissioning of the tracking station. Below, the top half of the PIKE environmental shelter is lifted in order to deconstruct the antenna on July 10, 2015. Since PIKE was no longer operational, equipment was removed and repurposed by the U.S. Navy Research Laboratory. (*United States Air Force 140919-F-WR604-014/50713-F-PD986-170*)

CURIOUS COMMUNITY MEMBERS ENGAGE WITH SCHRIEVER AIRMEN: Above, Captain Angela Tomasek (right), 2 SOPS engineering flight commander, briefs Colonel Nicole Malachowski (retired) (center, standing), while Senior Airman Sean Romm, 2 SOPS space systems operator, monitors a satellite health on December 19, 2019. Malachowski was the first female Thunderbird pilot and spent twenty-one years in the USAF. Below, Girl of the West Sierra Silva and the aide to the Girl of the West Kayla Summers hand out Chik-fil-A chicken sandwiches to Schriever airmen on June 29, 2018. The Girls of the West visited the base to increase awareness of the 2018 Pikes Peak or Bust Rodeo (July 11–14), along with raising awareness and support for local military and their families. (*United States Air Force 191219-F-UM970-0006/180629-F-IX728-1138*)

Another Day at Schriever ... Another Group of Visitors: Above, Captain Jeffrey Wagner, 2 SOPS mission commander, briefs the squadron mission to a tour group of motion picture and television directors, producers and writers on July 17, 2017. A sound understanding of space missions and their operators provides more accurate realism in film productions. Below, Colonel Kent Taylor (rear, standing), vice commander of the Space Warfare Center, describes Desert Storm-era space operations to members of the joint civilian orientation course inside the JNIC conference room. Historical perspective of space operations equally prepares government civilians to execute their duties and support the nation. (*United States Air Force 170717-F-WR604-0023/ National Archives DF-SD-07-08144*)

NOTHING STOPS SCHRIEVER'S DEFENDERS: Above, Airman First Class Joseph Snyder, 50 SFS, fights the bitter Colorado cold to wave cars onto base. Security forces help protect the multi-billion-dollar installation and its thousands of workers and are a critical part of the base's workforce. Below, Staff Sergeant Alton Johnson responds to a report of a gunman during a recent operational readiness inspection exercise. Frequent training and exercise opportunities such as these help hone the skills of Schriever's defenders. (*National Archives DF-SD-02-02659/DF-SD-02-02654*)

START OF ANOTHER DAY ON THE GREAT PLAINS: Above, Airman First Class Bobby Shanklin guards critical infrastructure while armed with an M16 rifle. Shanklin is a satellite systems operator with 3 SOPS but is also trained as a security forces augmentee when needed. Below is a shot of satellite antennae during sunrise on the Colorado prairie. Each day, hundreds of satellite contacts are transmitted through dishes like these around Schreiver AFB to orbital assets providing top cover for the nation and assisting American soldiers, sailors, marines, airmen, and guardians in defending freedom around the globe. (*National Archives DF-SD-02-02657/DF-SD-02-02660*)

ENTERTAINMENT AND SUPPORT FOR THE TROOPS: Above, Senior Airman William Steward performs Luther Vandross' "Dance with my Father" at the 50 SW Celebration of Arts, February 24, 2007. Airman Steward is assigned to the 50th Operations Group standardization and evaluations division. Performers from on- and off-base honored African American artists such as Maya Angelou, Stevie Wonder, and the Temptations. Below, satellite dish dining facility staff pose for a photo in front of the 50 SW Headquarters building after winning the 2014 Air Force Space Command Hennessy award on January 2, 2015. The USAF-level award was established in 1957 and named after John L. Hennessy, a hotel and restaurant executive who led a special Hoover Commission task group advisory of military food service and commissaries board to improve military food service. The John L. Hennessy Award is named in his honor, promoting food service excellence between the military and industry experts. (*United States Air Force 070223-F-2661B-041/150122-F-WR064-001*)

FORMATIONS AND FITNESS—ALL IN A DAY'S WORK: Above, airmen salute in formation during the opening ceremony for the base's third annual Schriever Week event on September 26, 2016. The ceremony kicked-off events celebrating the base's thirty-first birthday, and the base community in general, with recreational and community-based activities concluding with a "Wing Warrior" run and a chief's barbeque. Below, 50 SW members enjoy a formation run around the base's restricted area, as a satellite antenna environmental shelter looms large on the horizon. *(United States Air Force 160926-F-JY173-002/50th Space Wing Public Affairs)*

TIERRA VISTA BASE HOUSING: Above, an overhead view of Schriever's first row of company grade officer base housing in October 2009. The base's restricted operations area sits in the background. Prior to the completion of base housing, military members lived at Peterson AFB or on the economy in Colorado Springs. Safety during winter months and ability to recall personnel during crises were a few of the reasons for the construction of housing on base. Below, Second Lieutenant Caleb Murphy and his wife Christina stand on their new front porch in Tierra Vista's new base housing, complete with four bedrooms and energy efficient appliances. (*United States Air Force 091006-F-0000A-686/ 090826-F-6340W-059*)

KEEPING SCHRIEVER PERSONNEL SAFE: Above, trainees belonging to the El Paso County SWAT team practice barricading the window of a vacant home in the Tierra Vista Community on Friday, August 11, 2017. Trainees practiced scenarios, such as capturing a suspect and securing the house perimeter. Events such as this allow cooperative engagements between base and local law enforcement in the case one is required to assist the other. Below, wing leadership and members of security forces celebrate the opening of West Gate's new canopy, October 17, 2011. The canopy provides environmental protection from the snow and rain frequent in Colorado. Heating elements that run the length of the roof warm the on-duty security forces from harsh temperatures. *(United States Air Force 170811-F-QZ963-0002/111017-F-XT791-001)*

3 SOPS Gets Ready for the Future: Above, Lieutenant Colonel Kevin Mortensen, 3 SOPS commander, takes a simulated swing during the ceremonial deactivation of Space Operations Center 32 on October 20, 2011. The demolition and upgrade were in preparation for the construction of the integration operations environment (IOE) for global MILSATCOM. Below, Senior Airman Les Brown, 3 SOPS DSCS operator, performs a state of health contact on the DSCS III satellite B6 on August 27, 2013, just days before its tenth anniversary on orbit. Since the DSCS III constellation was planned for the space shuttle, launch delays forced deployment on expendable rockets and allowed a number of DSCS III satellites to undergo a service life extension program to upgrade outdated electronics. (*United States Air Force 111020-F-WR604-020/130827-F-JY173-002*)

Continuing Comms to the Warfighter: Above, 3 SOPS Commander Lieutenant Colonel Chris Todd (center) accepts satellite command authority for the wideband global SATCOM-7 (WGS-7) satellite on October 13, 2015. The integrated circular IOE floor supported 3 SOPS and 4 SOPS simultaneously, adding efficiencies that led to a merged mission and the inactivation of 3 SOPS in 2017. Below, Lieutenant Colonel Armon Lansing (right), 4 SOPS commander, accepts the key from Colonel David Ashley, space and missile center AEHF program manager, signifying the handoff of the AEHF-4 satellite to the squadron on May 3, 2019. AEHF-4 joined the other high data-rate military satellite communication satellites supporting space and intelligence, nuclear and defense, theater mission defense, and special operations. (*United States Air Force 151013-F-JY173-001/190503-F-UM970-0005*)

TWO GENERATIONS OF WING COMMANDERS: Above, Lieutenant General Larry James (third from left) is welcomed by Todd Garcia and Mike Kondus of Actus Land Lease and Colonel Cary Chun, 50 SW commander, during a visit to Schriever's new base housing construction area on January 22, 2009. General James was a previous 50 SW commander from April 2001 to February 2003. Below, commander of Air Force Space Command General C. Robert Kehler received a demonstration of the GPS readily available navigation datalink (GRAND), a program that transfers GPS performance information through Milstar during a tour on May 13, 2008. (*United States Air Force 090122-F-6113F-007/ 080513-F-8010M-056*)

PROUD SCHRIEVER AIRMEN: Above, members of the 50th Operations Support Squadron participate in an open ranks inspection in front of the DeKok building on August 21, 2018. The squadron's approximately 120 airmen formed up in their Class B dress blues uniform while Lt. Col. David Gallagher, commander of the 50th OSS, inspected everyone. Below, Mrs. Carolyn DeKok (left) speaks to 50 SW airmen on October 22, 2008, to commemorate the fourth anniversary of name dedication ceremony for Building 210, as Colonel Cary Chun looks on. The 50 SW Headquarters was renamed after her husband, the late Lieutenant General Roger DeKok (1947–2003), the first commander of the 50 SW. (*United States Air Force 180821-F-WR604-0021/081022-F-1103D-006*)

50 SW LEADERSHIP (2013–2017): Above, Colonel William Liquori gestures to the audience after assuming command of the 50 SW from Colonel James Ross on July 11, 2013. Liquori's early assignments were at Falcon AFS with 3 SOPS, flying the UHF Follow-On (UFO) communications satellite, before transitioning to Onizuka AFS (CA) for work with NRO Operating Division 4 (OD-4) as executive officer. Below, Lieutenant General John Raymond (right), commander of the joint functional component command for space, passes the guidon to Colonel DeAnna M. Burt during the change-of-command ceremony on May 29, 2015. Taking command of the 50 SW, Colonel Burt was given responsibility for more than 4,200 military, civilian, and contractor personnel at fourteen worldwide operating locations, supporting operations for approximately sixty-nine surveillance, navigation and timing, space situational awareness, and communication satellites valued at more than $66 billion. *(United States Air Force 130711-F-WR604-001 /150529-F-WR604-032)*

Leadership Across the Spectrum: Above, 50 SW Commander Colonel Jennifer L. Grant hams it up for the camera during her brigadier general confirmation celebration on January 7, 2019. Below, Colonel James Smith, 50 SW commander, addresses the Veterans Day appreciation event in Ellicott, Colorado, on November 7, 2019. Smith began his career as a GPS spacecraft systems analyst in 1999, later becoming the first commander of the Peterson-Schriever Garrison, a USSF command replacing the 50th and 21st Space Wings. (*United States Air Force 190107-F-WR604-0021/ 191107-F-UM970-0009*)

SIGNS THEY ARE A-CHANGIN': Above, the front entry sign at the Schriever's main gate shows the major tenant units on the installation, *c.* 2004. A little over a decade and a half later, only one organization (310th Space Group) remains without major change. Air Force Space Command became the core of the United States Space Force in 2019; pieces of the 50th Space Wing have become Space Delta 6 (Satellite Control Network), 8 (Satellite Communications), and 9 (Orbital Warfare); the SWC (later renamed Space Innovation & Development Center) was disestablished, and the JNIC became the Missile Defense Integration and Operations Center for the Missile Defense Agency. Below, 50th Civil Engineering Squadron structural journeymen Senior Airman Trevor Jones (left, with helmet) and Staff Sergeant Kyle Burkepuertas (right), remove the 50 SW logo and title from the entrance of Building 300 on July 24, 2020. The signage was removed immediately following the deactivation of the 50 SW and alignment of Schriever as a part of the Peterson-Schriever Space Garrison. (*National Archives DF-SD-07-33645/United States Air Force 200724-F-WR604-0006*)

LEGACY CHANGES THROUGHOUT THE FORCE: Above, the emblem of the Peterson-Schriever Garrison displays a creature in the style of the mythological Lernaean Hydra, with each of the six heads representing a space force installation under its command: Peterson Space Force Base, Schriever Space Force Base, and Cheyenne Mountain Space Force Station in Colorado, Thule Air Base in Greenland, New Boston Space Force Station in New Hampshire, and Kaena Point Space Force Station in Hawaii. Below, seventy-three Peterson-Schriever Garrison officer and enlisted space professionals are administered the oath of office and oath of enlistment by Chief of Space Operations General John Raymond during a U.S. Space Force transfer ceremony on September 15, 2020. (*Department of Defense 200915-F-SK775-1045*)

NATIONAL SPACE DEFENSE CENTER AND JOINT TASK FORCE—SPACE DEFENSE: The National Space Defense Center (emblem above) was initially established on October 1, 2015, as the Joint Interagency Combined Space Operations Center (JICSpOC). The center was intended to improve processes and procedures, ensuring data fusion among DoD, intelligence community, interagency, allied and commercial space entities. On April 1, 2017, the JICSpOC was re-designated as the NSDC to better clarify its role and eliminate confusion with the Joint Space Operations Center (JSpOC). Below is the emblem of joint task force space defense (JTF-SD). JTF-SD is a joint task force responsible for executing control of space defense and space domain awareness units to protect and defend U.S. space capabilities. JTF-SD utilizes NSDC infrastructure to accomplish their mission of "Protect and Defend." (*Department of Defense*)

NSDC's SMSgt H. Robert Mosley Operations Floor: On July 9, 2019, the NSDC dedicated its operations floor (above) and a warfighter library to Senior Master Sergeant Harold Robert Mosley II. Mosley was the NSDC's senior enlisted leader in 2018. He died on November 23, 2018, in a rock-climbing accident. Below, Amanda Mosley and NSDC plans division chief Lieutenant Colonel Anthony Zilinsky lay a wreath during a retreat ceremony honoring her husband at Schriever AFB, on May 22, 2019. (*United States Air Force 190709-F-UM970-0024/190522-F-WR604-0002*)

Activation of JTF-SD: On October 21, 2019, then-Air Force General John Raymond (left), U.S. Space Command commander, presents the colors to U.S. Army Brigadier General Thomas James, recognizing the establishment of the joint task force space defense (JTF-SD) and James' selection as its first commander. Raymond would later become the first chief of space operations for the United States Space Force. Below, JTF-SD members—joint service military, civilian, and contractor—pose for a group photo on the NSDC operations floor. The JTF-SD enables unified action with interagency and international mission partners, deters aggression across the space domain, defends capabilities, and defeats adversaries throughout the continuum of conflict. (*Department of Defense #191021-D-IX214-1002/United States Space Force 210204-F-WR604-0010*)

SECOND BIRTHDAY CELEBRATION FOR SPACE FORCE: Above, a USSF member monitors space situational awareness from inside the NSDC. Below, Chief Master Sergeant Jacob Simmons (left), JTF-SD command senior enlisted leader, and NSDC Director Colonel Scott Brodeur (center background) continues the tradition of toasting the newest U.S. armed service with red plastic cups during the organization's Space Force second birthday celebration at the National Space Defense Center on Schriever Space Force Base, Colorado, on December 20, 2021. The origins of the USSF tradition are unknown, but a country music star once crooned, "Now, red Solo cup is the best receptacle/For barbecues, tailgates, fairs, and festivals," while disparaging his audience from drinking with a glass. (*United States Space Force 210204-F-UM970-0003/211220-F-WR604-0005*)

NEXT GENERATION SPACE WARRIOR THREADS: Above, the USSF lettering on the Operational Camouflage Pattern shows the service's distinct blue thread. Air force airmen who transfer into the U.S. Space Force will continue to wear the operational camouflage pattern utility uniform currently worn by USAF and U.S. Army personnel. Below, Major Dylan Caudill, model for the U.S. Space Force prototype uniform, describes the new material and cut of the service dress uniform at Schriever Space Force Base on October 19, 2021. (*United States Space Force 200422-N-WU045-0001/211019-F-WR604-0002*)

A NEW ERA OF SPACE OPERATIONS: Above, United States Space Force (USSF) Second Lieutenant Zachary Warlick (center) accomplishes his in-processing requirements with finance while Airman First Class Vlada Iakovenko, 50th Comptroller Squadron financial operations technician (left), guides him through the process at Schriever AFB on June 22, 2020. After graduating from the U.S. Air Force Academy and earning his USSF commission, Warlick is the first member of the USSF to be assigned to Schriever. Below, Schriever Air Force Base, Peterson Air Force Base and Cheyenne Mountain Air Force Station received new designations as Space Force installations during a renaming ceremony on July 26, 2021. This Department of the Air Force initiative aimed at establishing a unique identity and culture within the U.S. Space Force, the nation's newest military branch. (*United States Space Force 200622-F-PJ004-1016/210726-F-SK775-1102*)

BIBLIOGRAPHY

Department of the Air Force, *Environmental Impact Analysis Process: Consolidated Space Operations Center* (Washington, D.C.: Office of the Secretary of the Air Force, January 1981), books.google.com/books/download/Consolidated_Space_Operations_Center_MT.pdf?id=49w3AQAAMAAJ&output=pdf

Freeland, G. and Scardera, M., "The Death and Resurrection of NAVSTAR 6," 42nd Congress of the International Astronautical Federation (Montreal, Canada, 1991), archive.org/details/the-death-and-resurrection-of-navstar-6

Government Accountability Office, "Consolidated Space Operations Center Lacks Adequate DOD Planning," MASAD-82-14 (Washington, D.C., January 1982), gao.gov/assets/masad-82-14.pdf

--. "The Consolidated Space Operations Center Is Not Supported by Adequate Defense Department Planning," B-205335 (Washington, D.C., March 1982) gao.gov/assets/b-205335.pdf

--. "Consolidated Space Operations Center" (Washington, D.C., June 1982), gao.gov/assets/118811.pdf.

Hoffecker, J. F., Whorton, M., and Buechler, C. R., *Cold War Historic Properties of the 21st Space Wing* (Peterson AFB, CO: Air Force Space Command History Office, 1996)

Kaplan, E. and Hegarty, C., *Understanding GPS: Principles and Applications, 3rd Edition* (Norwood, MA: Artech House, Inc., 2017)

McMillin, S., "Future of Springs-based military activities remains bright," *Colorado Springs Gazette Telegraph* (January 11, 1987)

--. "Ground Broken for Hub of SDI Test Facility," *Colorado Springs Gazette Telegraph* (March 24, 1988)

--. "CSOC wants 5,107 acres to erect security corridor," *Colorado Springs Gazette Telegraph* (February 7, 1984)

Saunders, R. J., *Schriever Air Force Base: A History in Pictures* (Schriever AFB, CO: 50th Space Wing History Office)

Shaw, F. J. (ed.), *Locating Air Force Base Sites: History's Legacy* (Washington, D.C.: Air Force history and Museums Program, 2004), amc.af.mil/Portals/12/documents/AFD-131018-055.pdf.

Spires, D. N., *Beyond Horizons: A Half Century of Air Force Space Leadership* (Colorado Springs, CO: Air Force Space Command, 1998), apps.dtic.mil/sti/pdfs/ADA355572.pdf.

Sheehan, N., *A Fiery Peace in a Cold War: Bernard Schriever and the Ultimate Weapon* (New York: Random House, 2009)

Wooden, W. H., "NAVSTAR Global Positioning System Overview" (Washington, D.C.: Defense Mapping Agency, 1984), apps.dtic.mil/sti/pdfs/ADA140793.pdf.

INDEX

About the Author

Joseph ("Joe") T. Page II is a space historian and former USAF space and missile officer. The space and history "bug" bit him early in life while growing up at White Sands Missile Range, New Mexico—the "Birthplace of America's Missile and Space Activity." After spending a decade in uniform, Joe and his family finally settled in Albuquerque, New Mexico. He holds two bachelors of arts degrees from the University of New Mexico—in history and English—and is currently pursuing graduate studies in history.

While Joe is the author of a number of titles in Arcadia Publishing's "Images of America" series, focusing on military aviation and space history, this is his second Fonthill Media title.